745·5924

A Hug of
TEDDY BEARS

PETER BULL

in collaboration with

Enid Irving

THE HERBERT PRESS

First published in
Great Britain 1984
by The Herbert Press Limited
46 Northchurch Road,
London N1 4EJ

Designed by Enid Irving
Typeset in Great Britain by
Butler & Tanner Ltd, Frome and
London
Printed and bound in
Hong Kong by
South China Printing Co.

**British Library Cataloguing in
Publication Data:**

Bull, Peter, *1912–*
   A hug of teddy bears.
   1. Teddy bears
   I. Title   II. Irving, Enid
   745.592'4   GV1220.7

ISBN 0-906969-43-3

*For Ray who gave me the
Teddy Bear Clock on page 96
and very much else, with
love and gratitude.
Also for Enid's twins, Suzy & Max,
who somehow never had Teddies, until
they were quite old!*

Contents

A Hug of Teddy Bears

Sculpture of
President Theodore Roosevelt
by Steven Lasley, New York

This book is an attempt to convey to any non-believers the charm, loyalty and enduring qualities of one of the world's remarkable phenomena. The believers can just skip the text and take a peek at the pretty pictures.

'Oh lawks! He's at it again', I can hear my friends exclaim when they hear about this volume. It must seem to them that I have never had any other career than living on the immoral earnings of Teddy Bears. They are not, of course, really 'immoral'; but it must appear a parasitical life, in spending all my time whizzing around the world attending Teddy Bear Conventions, writing books about them, and sending the more talented members of my collection out to work.

Aloysius (né Delicatessen), the star of the television series *Brideshead Revisited*, goes out on modelling jobs, does guest spots on chat shows and is in high demand with American ladies touring the stately homes of England, who like to take tea with him as a final dotty treat.

Bully Bear, his direct descendant, has been kept busy both in fact and fiction. He also does a bit of modelling, and in his literary career, since holding up Lady Diana's train at The Wedding, he has been through quite a lot – everything from a rather alarming punk phase to leading a fact-finding expedition to Australia. This was to settle an agelong and controversial argument as to whether Koalas can qualify as Teddy Bears. The answer to that, incidentally, is a definite 'NO', though when I was at a Rally in Sydney several of the creatures entered the competitions in heavy disguises. I am happy to report that Bully settled what might have turned into an ugly situation in a thoroughly diplomatic and professional way, with no loss of fur on either side.

People often ask me when I became a collector. In actual fact I've never been one. The bears have just arrived as presents from kind persons. I now have around three hundred and fifty. Some, like myself, are Resident Aliens of America, and are cared for by suitable sitters-in. But you can only really love and rely on one special bear to share your joys and sorrows. Mine you will find on page 31. And I don't intend to fill up this introduction with a lot of the sentimental stuff about 'him', with which some of you are only too familiar.

Other facts on which I shall not dwell for long are How It All Started and who was responsible for the first Teddy Bear. It may seem surprising, but I really have only the faintest idea – and that certainly would not stand up in a court of law. You can learn all about the eighty-year-old controversy in other books, including some by me. Suffice it to say here

Hazel Pollock and Friend

that a likely beginning is illustrated on page 4. Theodore Roosevelt didn't, of course, actually pick up a little bear in his arms, but the picture makes a change from the cartoon by Clifford Berryman that anyone versed in Teddy Bear legend will be familiar with (see page 57). It appeared (that cartoon) in the *Washington Star* on 18 November 1902, and showed the President refusing to shoot a bear emerging from the forest. Roosevelt was on a political trip Down South, and the drawing was entitled 'Drawing the Line in Mississippi', which of course had a double (or even treble) meaning, as he was settling a boundary dispute at the time. It is believed that the cartoon inspired a toymaker in Brooklyn called Michtom to make a model of the little bear which very quickly caught the public fancy. Michtom wrote to the President asking him if he could use his nickname, 'Teddy'. Unfortunately the letter giving permission has been lost, which has caused other claimants to the title of Creator of the Teddy Bear to come forward. I am remaining completely non-committal after years of research. However, Mr Michtom was enabled to start the immensely successful Ideal Toy Corporation on the strength of his claim.

To return to this slim volume by its fattish author. One of its aims is to serve as a sort of love letter to the Teddy Bear himself, and it is far less boring to show a lot of pictorial truths than yack on about the psychological aspects of the whole mystique and the reasons for its triumphant survival.

The mystique lies in the faces of the bears themselves. As you flip or caress your way through the book you will probably become far wiser about the whole thing than I am, who have got rather confused and lost in the sudden and quite sensational rise in popularity of the Teddy. Spacemen and E.T.s may come and go but he goes on for ever. Or so it would seem.

Not that I don't think that it has now all gone a tidge too far. There are bears made to resemble famous personalities, either alive or dead, sometimes with a witty play of words on the name, like Humphrey Beargart, William Shakesbear or Bjorn Bearg. Granted that these highly original variations on a theme are intended mainly for the collector, children must get deeply confused. I am all for new ideas and, if someone wants a Teddy Bear entirely constructed from mink at the cost of a thousand dollars or more, why shouldn't they have him, and I gather these are in high demand. But the gimmicky Teddy is not for me. In my opinion the primary function of the Bear is to listen, not to recite the Declaration of Independence.

Somebody inevitably will ask, 'And what about the Growler?' Certain Teddies in the old days, and even recently, were fitted with a mechanism which, when pressed, emitted a low but friendly growl. Its principal use, I am sure, was to say 'Yes' or 'No' to any child who wanted an important

Vera London with Grunter (who also appears on page 87)

decision about something. The bear never growled without pressure.

The moment Teddy does something of his own accord or starts Acting a Part, he seems to me to lose the whole strength of his presence and friendship. When you are feeling low and desperately want to confide in someone, no one will listen more attentively than Teddy. And I am not thinking only of children. One of the saddest duties I have to perform is to reassure elderly people who are disturbed about what will become of their loyal beloved friends of many years' standing, should anything happen to the so-called owner. Some even go to the length of leaving instructions in their will that they should be buried or cremated together.

Only the other day I had a letter which touched me deeply. A completely sane human being of eighty wrote and asked me if I was willing to give a home to a 'beloved destitute . . . After a long time of faithful service he has not deserved to be cast on the rubbish heap or the bonfire by my executors (a bank) or given to a jumble sale to be knocked about by rough children.'

I replied immediately that I would be delighted and proud to take the bear into my lodging-house for Bears of a Certain Age. Shortly afterwards he arrived in splendid condition, and he seems already to have settled down with some of my other distinguished bequests. You will find a picture of him among other Senior Citizens in this book, although I will not identify him for obvious reasons. Anyhow there is no need, as his friend attached a little label with his name and date of birth on it round his shoulders 'so that he can keep his identity'.

There are now in fact several organizations geared for this sort of sad problem, though obviously a private person, willing to take the responsibility, is always a preferable legatee. At the end of this book you will find a list of homes where elderly and Senior Citizen bears will be welcomed with open paws. In some they will be permanently on show for future generations to marvel at and admire, and in others they will lead a sort of club-like existence, reminiscing with contemporaries and, I suspect, showing off a bit.

Unfortunately one of the results of the current vogue for old Teddy Bears is that certain people have become aware of their monetary value. A recent sale at Sotheby's produced some remarkable figures. There is no doubt that there is a rich market for a vintage bear in mint condition. This has naturally led to a good deal of bartering on both sides of the Atlantic, to say nothing of endless searches through grandmothers' attics and visits to country sales. Many a tired old bear has found himself changing ownership several times in a few months. This is unsettling.

On the credit side, however, it must be admitted that some people who have ignored their childhood friends for many years have now restored

Big Edward and Bridget

Johnny Pitt with equestrian teddy

Dusty

them to a place of honour, at the foot of a bed or even *in* same, realizing at long last that they've been neglectful of a valuable and once treasured possession. I have noticed at Teddy Bear Rallies and competitions the pride with which adults present their entries for inspection. It is often difficult not to award a prize to them rather than to some child who, in theory, wants his or her Ted to win recognition even more.

You may have noticed that so far I have tended to use the words 'persons', 'people' or 'adults' rather than run the risk of being accused of discriminating between the sexes; but it will come as no surprise to the *afficionado* or Teddy lover that men are equally addicted and susceptible. When I think of the pangs of frustrated emotion I went through when my mother gave my beloved friend away to a jumble sale (rummage sale to Americans), while I was away at school, I realize how differently I would have behaved now. Instead of sulking and behaving towards the mater as if she were a murderess, I would have either clocked her one and/or howled the place down, tracked off to the jumble sale and rescued my Teddy. But in those days it was considered 'cissy' to be still attached at the age of sixteen to what was (and still is, in uninformed circles) erroneously referred to as 'a stuffed toy'.

Nowadays all that is changed. It is quite usual to hear a mature gentle-man bemoaning the fact that he never had a Teddy, and for his wife to go out surreptitiously to buy him one. I remember the wife of a much beloved British actor coming to me one Christmas and asking me if I could help her find a really old bear for her husband, who was extremely ill. He had seen her Teddy and sadly realized that he'd never possessed one. I was happy to pass on to him 'Dusty' (a bear with a theatrical background; he was discovered in a dustbin, went on the stage, and, although the play flopped, he got a notice in *The Times*). I like to think his cheerful disposition comforted his new owner during his last years.

Every now and then a smart-aleck of an interviewer on the television or in one of the other so-called media remarks at the outset that it seems rather childish to him or her to show such an interest in Teddy Bears. Keeping my cool, I reply that it doesn't seem any more childish to me than collecting cars, yachts or wives. The foolish interrogator is then apt to become rattled and ask what use they (the Teddies) are to the community. After that it's plain sailing for me.

I reply that they are very brave. He (or she) looks at me as if I've gone completely insane. I press on into the attack and explain that they have accompanied Battle of Britain Pilots into the air, soldiers in Vietnam, and have helped an Italian climber to conquer the Matterhorn.

'When did *you* last conquer the Matterhorn?' I find myself asking with a seraphic smile on my face. My interviewer is bereft of speech. I press on.

Hospital visiting

Pooh Street in Poland

'They help children in hospital by being beside them on their first night there. In fact,' I add, 'they have been known actually to save children's lives.' Then, if I'm feeling particularly beastly, I ask my inquisitor if he or she has saved any children's lives recently.

And of course I am speaking the truth, as many doctors and parents will testify. On other pages you will find more details as to how organizations like Good Bears of the World operate, and give such magnificent service. And I don't need to tell you how often in the advertising media a Teddy Bear is used as a symbol of security and comfort, whether it be to promote heating, lighting, sleeping pills or building societies.

During the fifteen years or so in which I have been connected with the dear creatures I have met many fascinating, warm and totally sane people. I can't remember meeting anyone interested in the phenomenon of the Teddy who was bitter, unpleasant or downright beastly. I even think there was probably something really rather nice, deep down, about that Russian lady spy who was deported from Britain clutching a large Teddy Bear.

Small talk in the Victorian Era was largely confined to the weather, what books were being read, what plays were being seen, etc. Then a couple of wars changed the trend and automatically new topics opened up. In the last post-war period astrology was always good for getting to know people (and what sign are YOU?). Now, for the more serious, the political situation and nuclear problems are to the forefront. But I am willing to bet that if anyone of any age in a group of four or more people were to mention a predilection for Teddy Bears, at least fifty per cent of those present would have a story about them to relate.

It must be admitted that the tightrope between sentimentality of the truest kind and mere whimsy is a thin and dangerous one, and I have to watch my step carefully. Thinking of the Russian for Winnie The Pooh is a good antidote. It happens to be Vinni-Pukh. I do sometimes see a look of dread come over the faces of some of my dearest friends when I start banging on about Teddy Bears. Yet I feel disloyal if I play it down.

Another antidote to excessive gooiness on the subject is that there is evidence of the existence of such things as evil Teddies, or ones which seem to exude the opposite of the usual qualities of the good, cuddly, comforting friend. Take 'Peter', for example, a German bear with fearsome teeth and a cruel face, who was given to me by Georgina Anka, then editor of the German toy magazine *Puppen und Spielen*. She was a delightful, generous lady and clearly thought she was giving me a great treasure. There were a few hundred 'Peters', found in a bombed-out building after the war, all stored in boot boxes. Because of their scarcity, they were soon to become Collectors' Items.

(continued on page 14)

Muffins for tea *by Pauline McMillan*

I love my little teddy hes got such a furry tummy and he likes me very much and He cuddles me in bed I love him So much. His name is Jim

Selina Howells 7yrs

Lee Pierce 7yrs.

I like my teddy bear very much and I found him at cornwall near the swings.

I have not got a teddy bear but I would like one like this

Elizabeth 7yrs.

James 7yrs

My teddy bear is a good teddy bear his name is called pinked we play games and he come in my bed and he cuddles up with me

Children and their bears

In the next few pages there are several examples of the intense, rather complicated relationship between young persons and their bears. Often it can be almost closer than the one they have with their parents. For he (or she) can enter a secret world with Teddy. No demands, no regulations and, above all, a sympathetic and understanding friend to have constantly at one's elbow.

'Whose woollen eyes looked sad or glad at me', as the Poet Laureate, Sir John Betjeman, put it so gracefully in his verse autobiography *Summoned by Bells*.

You will notice in these drawings by children of Rusthall Infants School, Tunbridge Wells, the vivid imagination used in portraying their idea not only of the Teddy they possess or would like to possess but also of themselves. It is fascinating that the bears have far more varied faces than their owners.

An advantage of a Teddy as a friend is that he will shoulder the blame for some misdemeanour committed by his owner. 'It wasn't me,' you will hear the child shout, 'it was Teddy. Naughty, naughty Teddy!' And often as not this blatant lie will be accompanied by a sharpish blow or a throw across the room. Later, with luck, you will see the child apologizing to his friend and asking for forgiveness, which is readily given.

Curiously enough the child's imagination doesn't usually extend to the naming of his or her Teddy. Time after time children come up to me during rallies and competitions and, in a conspiratorial tone, making sure that no one is listening, whisper the name of their chum in my ear. Nine times out of ten it is 'Teddy', announced as if it was the most unusual name in the bear world.

So it came as a refreshing shock when one kid said 'Disgusting' in a bold voice. When asked how this unattractive name had been chosen, he admitted that he had once thrown up over his furry friend; his mother had exclaimed 'Disgusting!' and somehow the name had stuck.

Nowadays, happily, it is not considered unusual to hang on to your Teddy Bear during adolescence. The sinister comment, 'You're too old for that sort of thing, dear,' is rarely heard, mainly because a large number of parents have themselves managed to hang on to *their* Teddies. Times have changed, as these lines from John Betjeman's *Uncollected Poems* show:

When nine, I hid you in the loft
*   And dared not let you share my bed;*
My father would have thought me soft,
*   Or so at least my mother said.*
She only then our secret knew,
And thus my guilty passion grew.

I like my big teddy bear. He is so nice and good. He is not naughty at all. I love him so much

Melissa Dutton 7yrs

I love my teddy bear
yes i do
yes i do
Hes soso furry
yes he is
yes he is
I love my teddy bear.

Sonya Gifford 7yrs

I love my little teddy bear. He's such a happy fellow. He loves going to the shops with me in his pushchair. At christmas time we pull our crackers. He's such a good boy. His name is Nipper.

Clara Higgs 7yrs

Christmas Trees and Teddies

Christmas is a very busy time for bears, who find themselves whisked from shop shelves and deposited in new homes. They are sometimes loved from the word 'go' but often ignored or despised if there is already a resident Teddy lurking around. Some parents make the hideous error of getting rid of an old, battered and possibly smelly but beloved bear and substituting a brand new extremely expensive one. A child of four could tell them this is nothing short of criminal.

The Christmas tree opposite is decorated every year by the Wichman family who live in Lexington, Kentucky. They are dear friends of mine and Theodore's. It was Miss Adrian Wichman who gave Theodore his most cherished and valuable possession – a stamp album containing only stamps with bears in it. It is bound in leather with his name embossed on the front and has a dedication to him drawn in exquisite calligraphy.

This picture taken in front of a California redwood tree about 55 years ago is of Jean Fenton with her bear Miss Fenton (see page 84)

John Betjeman with Archibald

(*continued from page 8*)

I put Peter with the other bears on a chair in the hall of my flat, and their response was immediate. At least three of them straight away fell off in terror, and I can swear that half a dozen others looked away into the middle distance. I then moved Peter to a niche of his own, more or less out of sight, and calm was restored to the community. But some of my friends said that he mustn't be left out of the Christmas festivities, so I let him join the rest of my lot for a few days. But I could sense that he wasn't welcome, even at the season of supposed goodwill to all bears. (Personally I find it the tetchiest time of year, when almost everyone, including myself, is willing to snap heads off at the drop of a hat. Particularly bus conductors, taxi-drivers, shop assistants and persons in box-offices.)

Anyhow, I heard that 'Peter' was much sought after by collectors in America, and last year I betrayed him, I'm afraid, for a bag of dollars. The tension in my building has noticeably lessened, and I am hugely relieved that he's thousands of miles away from my hug.

Sometimes Teddies find themselves the tool of an unscrupulous person and are forced to take part in some nefarious scheme. This was so when a bear found himself in court as one of the principal witnesses in a sensational divorce case. Willi Mayer, a wealthy industrialist, suspected that his wife was having an affair with his chief accountant on a skiing holiday in Switzerland. So he sent in, as a spy, an extremely cuddly and innocent-looking Teddy with a bouquet of red roses and a loving letter. In the bear's ear (unknown to the bear, of course) was a device which picked up not only every sound that emerged from Frau Mayer's bedroom, but a reference to the eighty thousand marks which had been withdrawn from her husband's account.

A similar device was used in England not so long ago, by a pretty ruthless lady, to drag a prominent peer of the realm through the mud.

I still feel some sort of angst when I go through Customs with my little lot. Luckily Aloysius, as an international Star, usually enables us to get v.i.p. treatment and sail through; but what will happen when his fickle public are no longer at the seat of custom, as it were? Well, perhaps we will have another Teddy constellation by then. But before A's sudden fame, I had to resort to all sorts of ploys. The most successful of these concerned the form you have to fill in and show when you disembark in America, declaring the value of goods bought abroad. You are allowed to put down 'Miscellaneous: Fifty Dollars' as a rough assessment.

I usually do this but, being a Resident Alien, I am always asked how long I've been out of the country. If my absence has been long, they tend to ask why I've only bought fifty dollars' worth of gifts. Depending on my not always accurate assessment of my inquisitor, I reply that I am very

Clarissa and James Mason's bear, The Pooh, leader of their hug

Barbara Cartland and her 'Prince of Teddies'

mean and haven't bought anybody anything. Sometimes this brings a faded grin, but usually a blank stare, followed by a snap question, 'What's the most valuable thing you've brought in?' I produce a tiny jewel box, open it and announce with a seraphic smile, 'The smallest Teddy Bear in the world!'

This pronunciamento so shocks and astounds the Customs officer that, following a string of expletives, I am hustled away as if I had imported the bubonic plague.

All this despite the fact that not very long ago a large Teddy was found lying on a bench in Rio de Janeiro Airport, containing five hundred and twelve pairs of nylon knickers and two hundred and ten dresses. It must also be admitted that in this connection Teddies have also been used for smuggling not only jewels but drugs as well.

Customs officials! Curiously enough I would probably never have embarked on any of this Teddy Bear caper if it hadn't been for a case of mistaken identity. Leueen MacGrath, a lovely actress and even lovelier friend, was four years old at the time and was carrying her Teddy on one of those chic trains which used to whizz through Europe in a puff of smoke. It had stopped at a frontier and the officials were examining all the passengers' personal luggage. Having checked her parents' belongings, they turned their attention to the child's, seized her furry friend, slit his throat and opened his stomach all the way down. You can well imagine little Leueen's grief. She recounted this story one evening in New York, when about five of us were discussing childhood traumas. I, of course, weighed in with the story of my mother's thoughtless act and another chap had an equally traumatic Teddy Bear experience to tell. After the 'i' had flown off my typewriter and I had decided to call a halt to any further autobiographies, I was subconsciously trying to find a fresh subject about which to write, and here surely was a solution. I found out that no one had delved deeply into the whole dotty mystique of what at first appeared to be a childhood toy and which, to my cost and years of hard labour, turned out to be a catacomb of psychology, therapy and universal appeal.

I have already dealt in previous books with these serious aspects of the phenomenon and don't intend now to dish out too many of the old conclusions. But I think it is fair to say that Britain and America have been the principal devotees of the Teddy Bear movement, with Germany a close third. But recently I have noticed a change. Possibly this is because there appears to be no class or age limit to people who succumb to the Teddy Bear's appeal. For now he has caught the imagination of other countries which, until recently, had never even heard of the dear creatures.

A Japanese magazine last year devoted an entire colour section to them, and the Swiss, Dutch and Scandinavian countries are showing great

A Swell

Will they never ring?

interest. It's only in Mediterranean countries that the gospel does not seem to have progressed very far. Perhaps that is because the inhabitants are unfamiliar with real bears, except in circuses and zoos, and it's a known fact that leopards and lions are child's play to train compared with a genuine bear. Live bears are treacherous and unpredictable and maintain poker faces. And it is interesting to note that though the Russians had toy bears long before any other country, they were all slightly forbidding, usually made of wood, and in no way cuddly.

But Royalty and American Presidents have always had a penchant for the Teddy. Prince Charles's favourite tune for a long time was 'The Teddy Bears' Picnic'. And I am indebted to the gloriously witty Arthur Marshall for reminding me of a curious anecdote about Queen Wilhelmina of Holland, who was an incredibly rich lady and could indulge in any whim. Apparently she had a passion for the same melody as Prince Charles, and at dawn a military band used to strike up this jolly tune below the royal bedroom. The melody was entrusted, as the day progressed, to a pianist, a string ensemble, a harmonium, a jazz-band, and a full symphony orchestra. Even a momentary silence and the absence of teddies picknicking produced regal frowns and pouts and sulks, so that the tune had to be hastily repeated for the two hundred and fiftieth time that day.

When we had the Celebriteddy Exhibition at the second Longleat Teddy Bear Rally, a fine array of notable bears put in an appearance for the special occasion. They lined up in the Long Gallery in state, and people passed by in awed silence, as if paying tribute to a deceased monarch. Some could hardly believe that the 'Iron Lady' (Britain's slightly intimidating Leader) had not only kept her friend but was willing to display 'Humphrey' to an admiring crowd. The Queen Mother and Princess Margaret sent their Teddies, and many Embassies, sports personalities and members of both Houses of Parliament were represented. It was interesting to note that at least half the male television Newscasters in Great Britain were afficionados, and indeed one of them confided to me that his seven Teddies watched him read the news every night.

In America Tom Snyder, who had a Teddy Bear as his emblem, proved a wonderful friend to me when he had his 'To-Morrow' show, and several times I flew over with my little lot to have a jolly good yack about it all. I hasten to add, in case by a freak of chance they happen to read this, that Messrs Cavett, Carson and Griffin were very sympathetic to my cause too.

American Presidents are famous for hanging on to their Teddies, though Teddy Roosevelt's daughter, the late Mrs Alice Longworth, confided to me that her father, who, let's face it, probably was responsible for the whole thing, didn't care for them at all, but realized that, as a political symbol, they could be invaluable. The same Mrs Longworth, then in her

Heather Chasen and Amanda Barrie with their bear Blossom

'T.B.', bought in Chicago in 1903

eighties, told me, when I went to visit her, not to bring any press or bears. She hated them both. I arrived at her house in Philadelphia Avenue in Washington, quaking in my shoes, and with Theodore in my pocket, to find a delightful welcome waiting for me, with English muffins and proper tea in a great silver teapot, hosted by an acute, wildly witty lady, who dished out acidulated comments on life and people. I explained to her that my visit was principally to check up on a story that the first Teddy Bears had been of German origin and were used to decorate her wedding cake. She confirmed by photograph and her rapier-like memory my theory that the story was totally untrue.

I referred briefly just now to the Longleat Rally. Since the two which took place there in 1979 and 1981, by courtesy of the Marquess and Marchioness of Bath, groups have been getting together all over the world and hardly a week goes by without a Teddy Bear function taking place somewhere. In practically all cases attendances have been under-estimated. I went to one last year where 1000 arctrophiles (Friends of the Bear) were expected and 10,000 popped in. I had warned them, so there! Luckily it was a fine day, and the Rally took place in a big park, but it cannot be emphasized too strongly to anyone organizing a T.B. Event that the underworld and closet owners will be turning up in force, come rain, hell or high water. It is also the surest way of making money for deserving charities, as many Good Bears of the World Dens will testify.

But, as Charity begins at home, I am going to end this introduction on a slightly sloppy note – though I hope also a practical one. If you are remotely impressed by the love and labour that has gone into the selection and contents of this book, think twice about the importance of Teddy Bears in other peoples' lives. I think the faces of all parties depicted will tell the story. And, though perhaps you cannot altogether understand or go with it, don't, if you are a parent, ever take away a Teddy from your child saying, 'You're too old for this sort of thing'. NO ONE IS TOO OLD. Repeat: NO ONE IS TOO OLD. Worse still is to tell him or her to give the beloved friend to a younger brother or sister. This course of action will lead to a real Cain and Abel situation.

Also, if you come across a bear by chance which you don't want personally, see that he (or she – there are lady bears) gets a home, even if it's in a hospital. If surgery is needed, there is a list on page 92 of doctors fully qualified to deal with this sort of thing. Failing these alternatives, just send the bear (collect) to me and I'll find him or her a home.

Teddy Bear persons are exceptional people and Enid Irving and I could not even have contemplated this book without the co-operation and kindness of Teddy lovers all over the world. A list of acknowledgements appears at the end and if, by chance, we have left anyone out, we apologize.

Matt Murphy

Matt Murphy has just thirteen hundred and seventeen bears. He has also been running banks ever since I first knew him two decades ago, and probably before that. Mark you, the bears in his collection are not all Teddies because Matt loves bears – period. In a comprehensive inventory which he sent me he listed what they were made of, and where they came from. There are fifteen gold, twenty silver and thirteen ivory ones, for starters. One hundred and ninety are made out of wood, while under the heading, 'Miscellaneous', I read leather, walrus tusk, pipe cleaners, rubber, soap, cork, straw, chocolate, sponge, whalebone, and mastodon tusk (natch). They come from all over the world – from one hundred and thirty-five countries.

Matt first became an arctophile at the age of six; he was in hospital and his parents gave him a dozen miniature German Teddy Bears. Unlike most collectors, he makes them and his other bears work, using his imagination to a fascinating extent. His pride and joy are two American Football teams who play games against each other throughout the season. They took part in eighty-four matches one season, and I was regaled with a highly technical description of the players' performances.

'Bear No 1, at Tight End,' (sometimes I think the British and American languages are poles apart) 'has kicked eighty-four field goals (252 points), two hundred and sixteen conversions (216 points) and caught thirty-six touchdown passes

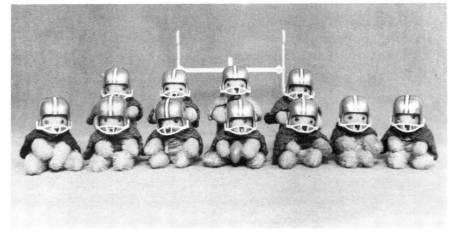

(216 points) for the 684-point total'. As a bonus bit of information he informed me that 'Bear No. 13 is not only a stellar Quarterback/Passer at football but a good tennis-player'.

He brought some of his football stars over to show me once when he was opening a new branch of the Bank of Montreal in London. They travelled in a very chic briefcase.

Matt seems to move house and banks rather often, and is now with Republic. If his branch wasn't situated in Plano, Texas, I would think very seriously of transferring my overdraft there.

Mrs Sanderson

Sybil Sanderson restored this bear herself. He was in a badly battered condition when she took him over. An astrologer of repute, she contributes a column to the popular *My Weekly* magazine. She is a dab hand at casting natal charts and has produced them not only for me and my friends but also for Theodore (Taurus) and Bully Bear (Aquarius). When we were running the Astrological Emporium (Zodiac) she was an enormous help and I followed her advice implicitly when Pauline McMillan and I produced *The Zodiac Bears*. Devoted to Theodore, she has deluged him with what the late Miss Joyce Grenfell would have described as Useful and Acceptable Gifts. A lot of the furniture in his bedroom (on page 34) was given by her and has his planetary signs inscribed on it, a fact of which he is inordinately proud and which makes him show off a tidge too much.

Mark Steele

Dozey Parker, special friend of Mark Steeke, who this year is into bicycling

I have been in correspondence with Mark for many years, but alas I have never met him, possibly because he spends most of his time flitting from New Zealand to Fiji and back. He is in fact head of the Fiji National Tourist Office but this doesn't prevent him from indulging in his devotion to the Teddy Bear world.

About ten years ago he staged the first Teddy Convention in New Zealand. He produces a publication called *The Bunratty Times* which comes out at least once a year and deals with Beariana. Mark was born in British Guiana (Guyana) where he spent the first twenty-eight years of his life. He has written two books in verse about his favourite bear, 'Littlejohn', who is (and I quote) 'only 6½ centimeters tall'. ('Only!', I heard my Theodore sniff when I typed that. He was looking over my shoulder. I don't think he knows what a centimeter is, frankly.)

The MacKinnon Bears

I seem to have known about Deirdre MacKinnon, her mother and their bears, since I started to write the first Teddy book. Their collection is now famous throughout the world, and at the end of this tome you can find out how to visit it and them.

The Wareham Bears

They live at 18 Church Street, Wareham, in Dorset, England, fifty yards from Lady St Mary's Church, and are the brainchild of Mary Hildesley and her husband. They are a tremendous attraction for visitors and tourists and a unique collection. They are a community, living in exquisite surroundings and in superb taste in a cellar of the Hildesleys' house. There are about seventy of them all told, among them some outstanding characters.

Havahug, a comfortable bear of few words, with no dress sense whatsover, is the cook, and her husband Havahand works in the stables (centre, below). Miss Pizzi Carter is very musical and is surrounded by knick-knacks. Her horrible nephew, Mac, is a great know-all. Another resident is Miss P. Nutt (centre), a retired Matron of a hospital for birds in Malaysia. She was able to converse with the Boat

People, some of whom are visitors.

Annabel de Trot (below, left), a law unto herself, is very naughty and likes being late and shocking people. Then there are Thomson, who changed his name from Gravy, and his friend Walker, who prefers not to wear clothes.

Magnus Humble, twin brother of Jack, has a very expensive car and many hangers-on. Mr and Mrs Gilbert look after the garden and a host of their friends, including Johnson and Parker, who are charismatic worms, and wear top hats. But perhaps the favourite and best-loved bear of all in the community is Little Mutt (above, left), who has one leg shorter than the other; she has to wear an orthopaedic boot. She is the bear who has all the good ideas. And now I've had one. Go and see the Wareham Bears if you are anywhere near Bournemouth.

The Roosevelt Bears

Evelyn Lovell, a charming lady antique dealer from Kentucky, specializes in quilts, toys and Teddy Bears. The only trouble is, she cannot bear to part with the Teddies. The pictures here show just a small selection of her unique collection of the Roosevelt Bears (*c.* 1902–9).

Bear blockbuster

Monday is wash-day

Now I lay me down to sleep, counting sheep

We've been working on the railroad . . .

Virginia Walker

She is one of the great personalities in the Teddy Bear World. A lovely, warm, larger-than-life character, who never misses a Rally, Convention, or indeed any Teddy which catches her fancy and which she can add to her immense collection. This is housed in 'Teddy Towers' in Florida. Her chief companion (in the bear world, I hasten to add, in order not to offend her family) is 'Eggie', an extremely energetic bear who travels with her all over the world.

He sees himself as a Great Power in the Teddy Bear fraternity, and has just published a magazine called *The Eggie Eagle*, which in format looks suspiciously like *The Teddy Tribune*, but not as thick. It would appear that Eggie is not only the Owner, Publisher, Editor and Contributing Editor, but also the Columnist of the magazine. A Virginia Walker is listed as Editorial Assistant and Business Manager.

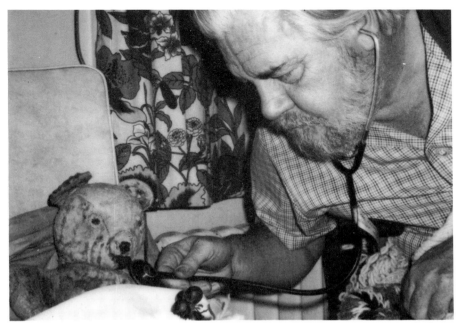

Alan Thomas

Alan's Teddy is seventy-three and Bournemouth Bear, his constant companion, is around sixty. As you can see, they are adventurous in the extreme. Alan, one of the most distinguished Antiquarian Booksellers in Britain, used to run a bookshop in Bournemouth and was a great friend and inspiration to the young Durrells, Lawrence and Gerald, during their early life, and indeed ever since.

Teddy and Bournemouth Bear in Tunisia at El Djem

Gerald Durrell

Here is an unlikely snap of the great naturalist preparing to inject a Teddy Bear against the threat of paw and mouth disease. The other photo

is of the late Pedro, the Bespectacled Bear, an exceptionally rare animal, who was one of the star attractions of Gerald Durrell's magnificent Zoo, run by the Jersey Wildlife Preservation Trust in the Channel Islands.

Once when I was staying there, Pedro had a desperate need to raise money (a) for a wife and (b) for a new and larger cage. Asking all the staff to turn a blind eye, I managed to collect a crowd by telling them that Pedro would execute a dainty waltz if they would pay to see such a phenomenon. In no time Pedro had a full house, and I plied him with chocolate bars, which made him dance with delight.

Gerald and his lovely American wife, Lee, interrupted their honeymoon to bring their Teddies to the first Longleat Rally in 1979.

You have a friend in Congress! Best Wishes Congressbear Percy.

Congressman Percy Bear

. . . and a few of his many chums.
From the top, working round the
page, are Backwards, Blondie,
Muffin and Little Pooh.

Steiff

Among the earliest bears are those
produced by this great German firm
of toy manufacturers. The Steiff
family have been operating for over
a hundred years but it wasn't until
1902–3 that Richard Steiff presented
their first bear at the Leipzig Fair.
The prototype was the result of
many experiments. A big order came
from America. 'Teddy' is not a
German word and until 1907, Steiff
bears were simply called 'bears'. But
their claim to have been fore-runners
of today's Teddies is a strong one.

Throughout this century Steiff
have produced beautiful examples of
our furry friend, though sometimes I
worry about the 'Knopf im Ohr'
(Button in the Ear) symbol which
has distinguished Steiff work since
1905.

The family is still closely
connected with the firm and there is

a museum at Giegen-on-the-Brenz which has a wonderful array of early Beariana. The archives are jealously guarded and a history of Steiff is currently being researched.

Doris and Terry Michaud

For the Michauds, it all began with The Professor (far right). They have been collecting old bears for many years and they acquired, during their search, a 1906 bear who reminded their daughter of one of her teachers. Hence the name, and over four hundred pretty senior Teddies.

Visiting Tim Atkins of 'The Bear Necessities' shop in Boston some years later, they bemoaned the fact that nobody made contemporary bears with the old characteristics. Terry and his wife then started to do exactly this.

Here you will see fine examples of their work and also some of the prototypes. They set up a sort of cottage industry, and two married daughters are part of the 'finishing off' team. They gave me a bear dressed as a newsboy carrying a bundle of papers (for real), who has given us all a great deal of pleasure and kept us abreast of the times.

The Michauds live in Midland, Michigan, and their firm is called Carrousel.

Ted Barber

Belonging jointly to Martin Hayward and his mother of Barnsley, this bear is aged 77. Martin has kindly supplied me with a fascinating biography:

'Bought for my grandfather in Manchester by his mother and father after a day at the races. For twenty-three years lived in Public Houses, viz: "The Sportsman" at Low Valley, Darfield, and "The Cross Keys" at Stairfoot, both of which my great-grandparents owned.

'Ted moved into a general dealer's shop in 1934 and went into the ownership of my mother. In 1936 he retired into a private residence (Council house) with her – the smallest house he has ever lived in.

'I was born in 1960 and from 1961 Ted has been jointly owned by myself and my mother. He was named after one of the regulars in the afore-mentioned pubs. Ted Barber himself, an ex-collier, also took the photograph around 1906–1907. In May this year [1984] my grandfather, the original owner, will be seventy-nine years old.'

Theodore

I think it is only right to devote some space to my small friend, Theodore. Certainly it is quite time to make a fresh assessment of the qualities which make him unique to me.

I said earlier that only one Teddy can take first place in one's affections, and despite the material success of such personalities as Aloysius and Bully Bear, Theodore is The One. He has been with me longer than any of the others, and was given to me to celebrate a first night by my friend, Maurice Kaufmann. I fear I took him for granted from the word 'go'. I have carried him in my pocket everywhere. He's only about four inches tall in his non-stockinged feet, so he doesn't take up much room. But travelling conditions are not ideal for him.

I suppose he's a symbol to me of unloneliness. Because I whizz about so much it is a great comfort to wake up in a strange bedroom and find a friendly and smiling face on the table beside me. Not that he's always in a good humour. For instance, he hates our trips to Greece, where I have a tiny house on a fairly remote island. He starts grizzling the moment we touch down on that lovely sunny land. It's partly because the Greeks don't understand about Teddy Bears unless they have had the luxury of a British Nanny.

He also finds it too hot out there, and quite often turns his head to the wall overnight on the shelf above my bed. He would dearly love to kick over the very small Greek-English lexicon he was given by an admirer.

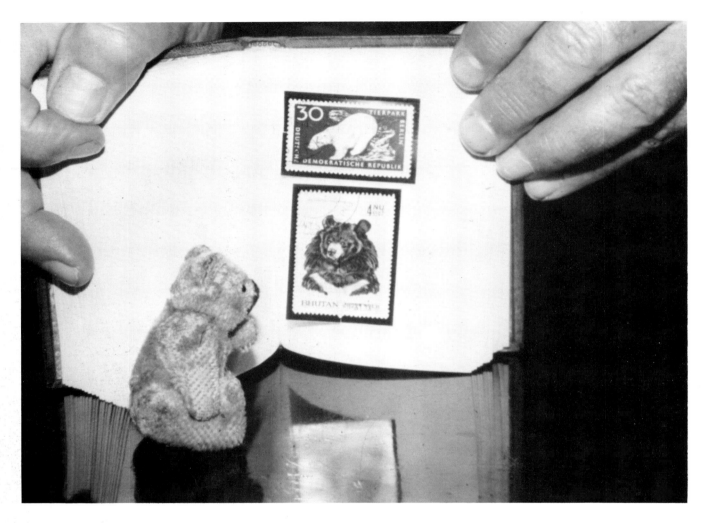

Of the latter he has plenty, and in his home on top of a bureau he has all his possessions stored, including an immensely valuable stamp album (nothing but ones with bears) and a lot of Japanese musical instruments.

On the following pages you will see that he's a Bear of Property and even has a shop to give him an income. The photographs were taken just after he'd returned from an exhausting tour of the States, which is why he is still in bed. Little does he realize that his friends have organized a concert to welcome him home and two pianists are waiting to beat the hell out of Bach. You will notice his closest friends are in the bedroom with him, including Booty Bear, given me by Don Busby, one of my partners, who doesn't seem to give a hoot about him being imprisoned in a boot.

There we must leave this small company of friends. It is difficult not to appear whimsical and over-sentimental about Theodore, but to me he is the embodiment of loyalty, friendship and complete understanding. And I don't care who knows it.

32

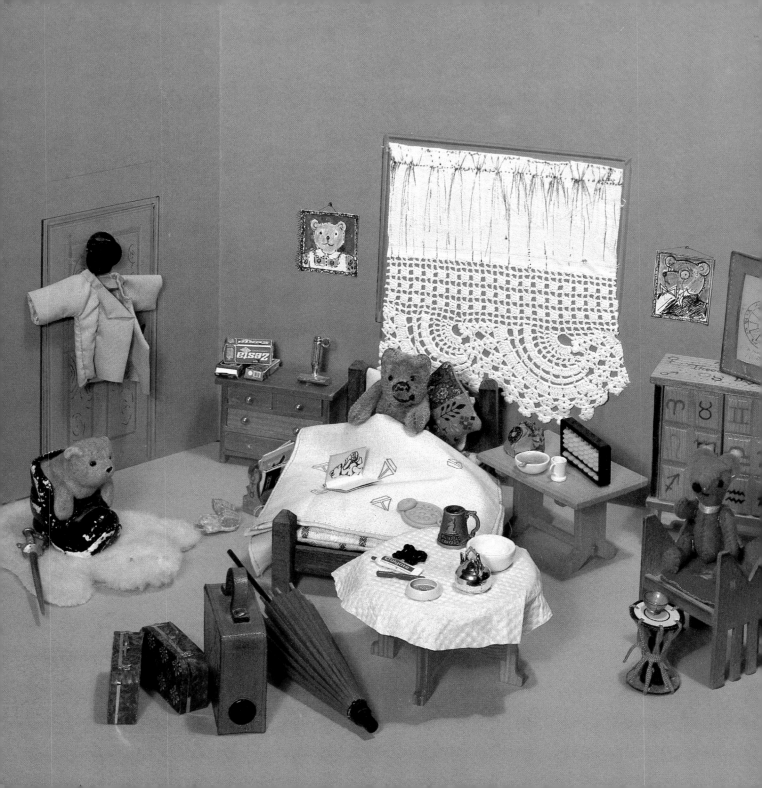

The Marquess
of Bath
and Clarence

When Lord Bath launched the first
of his two Teddy Bear Rallies at
Longleat, his magnificent Stately
Home, I don't think he realized
quite what a precedent he was
setting or, indeed, on acquiring
Clarence, what he was letting himself
in for.

In a recent letter his Lordship says:

OPPOSITE *The author with some of his hug*

Dear Peter,
You ask me if I mind if Longleat features in your book. Now, if you'd
asked me the same question three or four years ago I would have been able
to give you a definite 'yea' or 'nay'.
Now I am afraid things are different. Clarence has both 'the Vote' and
'the Veto'. I don't know how it happened but it somehow evolved ever
since his last trip abroad.
I am humiliated but I thought it best you should know.
Anyway he has graciously consented and I for once wholeheartedly
agree with him.
If you don't mind I haven't shown him your treatise 'Bully Bear
Interviews a Noble Teddy' because I know it will only increase his Ego
and it is inflated enough as it is, and he will only want to write a foreword
or some such thing.
As for me congratulations
Yours
Henry

Rupert Bear

Arguably the first fictional Teddy to capture the public taste was Rupert Bear, the small colourful figure with his yellow scarf and check trousers whom I seem to have known all my life. He first appeared in London's *Daily Express* in 1920, drawn and written about by Mary Tourtel, though the captions in verse were contributed by her husband, a sub-editor on the newspaper. A Rupert League was formed, but had become so unwieldy by 1935 that it had to be abandoned. About that time Miss Tourtel's sight began to fail and she had to stop working on Rupert. A worthy successor proved difficult to find but eventually A.A. Bestall was chosen. He carried on the work quite beautifully for nearly forty years until he retired, and the column is now drawn and written by Jim Henderson.

It has appeared every day for over sixty years and was only crowded out twice, once by a Churchill wartime speech and once by the death of Pope John. I was asked a few years ago to do a treatment of one of Rupert's adventures for an animated cartoon film for which Paul McCartney had composed a score. He is a real Rupert freak and owns a lot of the rights. Alas, my treatment was rejected, as was my contribution to the film in which I dubbed the voice of Podgy Pig, one of Rupert's

closest chums. Here are some extracts from one of the most imaginative adventures, *Rupert and the West Wind*.

The story tells how Rupert goes in search of the West Wind to blow away the winter fog. He is helped in his search by many friends, including the Professor, the Wise Old Goat, the messenger bird on whose back he flies to the Palace of the Four Winds, and a small zephyr, and finally discovers the West Wind lazing at home on a warm island. Reminded by Rupert of his duties, the West Wind flies back with him to dispel the fog and bring Spring to Nutwood, where Rupert lives.

Winnie-the-Pooh

Pooh

What is there Nooh to say about Pooh? Books have been written about his creator and about Christopher Robin Milne, whose early life was made intolerable by his association with his famous Teddy. He was mocked at school and for years after, and I can well understand his feelings about the whole thing.

All I can do is reiterate the unquestionable facts about what is possibly the most famous bear in the world. I am greatly indebted to my friend, Brian Sibley, who, apart from the aforementioned C.R. Milne, is the greatest expert on the whole subject, and certainly the least prejudiced. Two of the sketches you see here are from Brian's brilliantly constructed *Pooh Sketch Book* in which he put together all the ideas that Ernest Shepard later used in what has been one of the major factors in the astounding success of the books. Shepard's illustrations are indeed to me the one indisputably evocative and nostalgic note of the Pooh series.

I first met Brian Sibley during the festivities to celebrate the fiftieth anniversary of Winnie-the-Pooh. I appeared as narrator in his radio adaptation of the history of Pooh called *Three Cheers for Pooh*, and during this time I learned more about the legend than I could have believed possible.

It all started in 1920 when a good-looking young lady bought a Teddy Bear in the toy department at Harrods. It may come as a shock to some of you to learn that Pooh was first called Teddy Bear, and then

Edward Ditto. The lady was Dorothy Milne, the wife of Alan Alexander Milne, at that time an essayist and humorist, and regular contributor to *Punch*.

The bear was destined for the Milne son, who was then very young indeed, and made his first literary appearance in the Milne volume of light verse called *When We Were Very Young*, published in 1924 (it wasn't until 1926 that Winnie-the-Pooh was to have a book of his own). His success was instantaneous, and he

was even eventually to have a street in Poland named after him (page 8).

Without doubt one of the principal reasons for his phenomenal success was the way in which Shepard's drawings so perfectly matched the verse. Strangely enough, Milne who had come across Shepard when both worked for *Punch* was not keen on the idea of the collaboration at first, as he apparently disliked the artist's style. It was E.V. Lucas, a fellow essayist and verse-writer, who convinced

Milne that Shepard was the right man for the job. Milne was won over by some specimen drawings and the inimitable partnership was started.

Winnie-the-Pooh was followed in 1927 by a second book of verse, *Now We Are Six*, and in 1928 by Pooh's further adventures in *The House at Pooh Corner*. All were illustrated by Shepard, who presented his drawings to the nation when he died in 1976. They can be seen in the Victoria & Albert Museum, London.

At a sale at Sotheby's before his

Christopher Robin with Winnie-the-Pooh and Kanga in the 'Hollow Tree House' at Cotchford Farm, c. 1926

death one of his earlier sketches fetched £1,200 (in 1968 a considerable sum for this type of work). *Winnie-the-Pooh* sold over 300,000 copies in Great Britain alone in the first three years, and now has been translated into twenty languages, including Latin and Greek. *Winnie Ille Pu* (the Latin title) by Alexander Lennard was first published in Brazil, of all places. Pooh is known as Mici-Maco in Hungary, Joanica-Puff in Portugal and Kibus Puchaket in Poland.

The secret of his success? Christopher Robin Milne himself thought it was largely because the books were written to be read aloud, thus forming a bond between parent and child, which the latter remembered and repeated to his own offspring years later.

Over ten million hardbacks of the Pooh books were sold in America in the first twenty years, and in the *New York Times Book Review* it was still being reported quite recently as one of the best-selling children's books. In Britain the four books sell annually at least half a million copies, of which a third are sold to South Africa, Australia and New Zealand. Sydney University's Tiddleywinks Society (yes, really!) organized a Pooh Festival, and there is apparently a Pooh Society in New Zealand, where they play Poohsticks with real people, 'because the water is so warm'.

On the other hand Dorothy Parker wasn't so keen. Writing book reviews in *The New Yorker* under the pseudonym of 'Constant Reader', on reaching only page 5 of *The House of Pooh Corner* she announced 'Tonstant Weader Fwowed Up'.

But Pooh's appeal is everlasting.
Universities and colleges hold
seminars about him. Pooh Societies
abound all over the world; and
Poohsticks is still played at Teddy
Bear Rallies and picnics.

3 Cheers for Pooh!
(For Who?)
For Pooh—

Paddington

Born 1956 on Paddington Railway Station in London (that's the legend anyhow) and, as every adult and child knows, he had arrived there mysteriously from Peru, of all places. In actual fact Michael Bond, his creator, got the idea when he was carrying out some last-minute Christmas shopping at Selfridges and saw a lonely Teddy sitting on a shelf.

Paddington's rise to fame and popularity has been nothing short of sensational and a lot of his success is due to the first and original drawings of Peggy Fortnum. Of the bear himself, Michael Bond thinks some of his own characteristics are embodied in him, like love of marmalade and duffel coats. It took two years and around five publishers to see the full potential of his brain-child and now the range of merchandise, to say nothing of the cartoons and sale of books, are a tribute to his lasting popularity.

The label attached to him when found in the train terminus read 'Please Look After This Bear. Thank You.' He has proved himself fully capable of Looking After Himself (and indeed many others).

Michael Bond and Paddington with friends at Paddington Station 1978

Oliver Q. Dodger

Born in the Spinney in Slope-on-Rye. Age unknown or refuses to tell us. Left home early and went to London to seek fame and fortune. By a strange fate and, naturally, in the course of his duties, he was drawn to the tea-room at Selfridges, where he met a family called Batchelor. The association started uneasily because Mrs B. made some disparaging remarks about a hippy wig which, perhaps unwisely, Oliver had donned for the occasion.

However, an honorary aunt of the Batchelors, Erin O'Hara, intervened and, over a highish tea, invited the bear to Germany where they were all living at the time. The senior Batchelor was stationed at Buchshlag and it was here that Oliver became intent on furthering his career. He started classes at a fashion school but alas found he had No Aptitude for Design. Then he took up ballet, but, owing to an ankle injury, he couldn't dance his way to stardom, as young Michael Batchelor did.

It was in journalism that he found his metier. Every well-read bear will be familiar with his acerbic but accurate dispatches in *The Bearsville Courier*. He edged his way into becoming the Roving Reporter for this august paper and travels extensively in this capacity. His hobbies in *Who's Who in Bearland* are listed as skiing, sending Letters of Complaint to Various Departments, and Buying Clothes (for Himself).

He can be contacted for extra assignments c/o Mary Batchelor, Cedar Farm, Easterton, Wilts.

A Christmas shop window

This is only one of many rather specially decorated windows, which in 1983 won the prize for the shop with the best and most original display in Britain during the festive season. It belonged to the hundred-and-some-year-old shop, Weekes, in Tunbridge Wells. What was so unusual about their idea was that they organized a competition for children to guess how many Teddies were hidden in the window.

As it was a general store the results were electrifying, and for weeks (no pun intended) a paw, a bit of a head or a pad could be observed, if one looked very carefully, poking out behind anything from a gas fire to a nifty nightdress.

The establishment started as a small drapery and millinery shop in 1854 in the days of the Crimea and a Mr R.W. Weekes was one of the partners. He died in 1892 and his two sons E.B. and S.S. took over. In 1911 the shop was enlarged by the purchase of two licensed premises, The Bell Hotel, which now houses the curtain department and ladies' underwear, and later The Bridge Hotel, which is now the main entrance and stairway to all floors.

I had a wonderful time there presenting prizes to the children who had guessed the correct number of hidden Teddies and I am happy to report that among the directors of the highly individual emporium R.G. Weekes and S.G. Weekes still represent the family founder at the helm.

Teddy Edward VIB

Teddy Edward VIB (Very Important Bear) is a BBC TV star. He won the medal he always wears in a ski race, which distinguishes him from all other Teddy Bears. He is the most travelled teddy bear, having been to Mount Everest, Timbuctoo and the bottom of the Grand Canyon – you name it and he has probably been there. Photographed and written about by Patrick and Mollie Matthews, his books have sold over a million copies.

Arriving at Monument Valley in his jeep (opposite) just in time to put up his tent. Many cowboy and Indian films are made in this famous American desert.

The next day he went, in the saddle-bag of a mule, down to the Colorado River at the bottom of the Grand Canyon (above right). He has a certificate to prove it.

Teddy Edward travelled 500 miles down the River Niger in a canoe to Timbuctoo. This is one of the Southern Sahara desert markets he visited (below left).

From Khatmandu, the capital of Nepal, Teddy Edward went to look at Mount Everest – the mountain with the white puffy cloud over it (below right).

Aloysius

Born 1907 in Sacco, Maine, USA. Sat on the shelf of a Dry Goods and Grocery store for fifty-five years. Presented to me in 1969 by the owner, Miss Euphemia Ladd, who thought her Teddy needed a change and liked the look of my little lot on the Johnny Carson show. On arrival in the Bull hug he was christened Delicatessen, not realizing that this was going to be changed by sensational events and deed poll in the seventies.

When the television series of Evelyn Waugh's novel *Brideshead Revisited* was first mooted by Granada it had never crossed our minds that we had a potential world star on our hands. At the audition (there were four other actors up for the part) Delicatessen romped home.

OPPOSITE *Anthony Andrews as Lord Sebastian Flyte with Aloysius on the river Cherwell, from Granada Television's* Brideshead Revisited
RIGHT *Anthony Andrews as Lord Sebastian Flyte, Diana Quick as Lady Julia Flyte, and Jeremy Irons as Charles Ryder, with Aloysius outside Castle Howard, Yorkshire, on location for* Brideshead Revisited

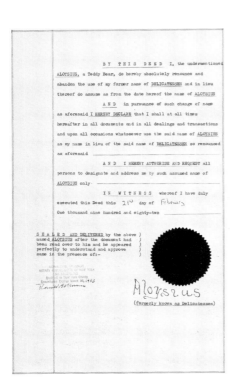

In the television film he scored a
notable success. He even won an
award from the magazine *Time Out*
'for the best performance in most
trying circumstances'. This pleased
him greatly. Delicatessen became
Aloysius.

But, alas, travelling to the States
in Concorde, being photographed
nude by a swimming-pool in
Hollywood, and having his pads
imprinted in the cement outside
Grauman's Chinese Theatre went
slightly to his head. All this glamour
was not helped by the countless
television scenes with Lord Sebastian
Flyte, which involved a good deal of
alcoholic intake. Not having
Anthony Andrews' experience as an

career at that moment.

'What on earth do you mean?' I asked innocently.

'Well,' replied Mr Granger, 'he's going on location to Venice with Lord Olivier on Tuesday, and he might pick up some hints on acting.' He has.

actor (Mr A gave an unforgettable performance as the unhappy Sebastian), Aloysius found himself becoming more and more at the mercy of the bottle. Eventually he was persuaded to join Alcoholics Anonymous (Teddy Bear Branch).

He has now settled down peacefully in the King's Road, Chelsea, does occasional modelling jobs and makes guest appearances on chat (or growl) shows. Throughout the television series he was treated with the utmost courtesy by everybody on location and was referred to always as 'the artiste'. In fact when I wanted the artiste's services for 'An Evening of Bull' Derek Granger, the producer of *Brideshead*, told me rather sharply that I couldn't interfere with his

I would like to point out, as a bit of absolutely useless information, that my friend Christopher Sykes, who took the stunning photograph of Aloysius in the punt, had a dog called Bully. He was a bulldog.

Bully Bear

Born 1981, Winscombe, Avon, England. A direct descendant of Aloysius (Delicatessen). I was approached by Jack Wilson, Managing Director of the House of Nisbet, as to whether I would be interested in being associated with his firm in the manufacture of a new type of Teddy Bear. He had been tipped off by that marvellous P.R. lady, Dawn Allan, who specializes in toys, that I disapproved of the modern Teddy. Anyhow, Jack Wilson and I seemed to hit it off, and his wife Alison and I designed a bear which combined all the old-fashioned essentials (viz: snout, hump and markings on paws and pads) with a slightly trendy and mischievous look. We did tend to model him on Aloysius, and we

christened him Bully Bear. It was then that I went one step further. The bear had such obvious personality that I decided to write some little stories about him. I found an ideal collaborator, Enid Irving, to do the drawings, and we started off by sending him to the Royal Wedding to carry the Royal train.

After that he went to the Longleat Rally, and became Punk for a brief period (a result of hearing himself described as 'a dear old-fashioned teddy-bear'). Then he got jealous of Aloysius's success and trotted off to Hollywood, thinking he would be asked to star in *The Hunchbear of Notre Dame*, but sadly ended up merely doing a commercial for peanut butter.

In the meantime the House of Nisbet had designed a Young Bully, smaller than the original Bully, but dressed in the regalia of the Worshipful Company of Peanut Butter Eaters. Bully Minor followed and there are even rumours of a Theodore-sized Bully in the offing.

Meanwhile the fictional Bully had redeemed himself somewhat by becoming a fairly unconventional doctor, and leading the expedition to Australia described earlier in this book. His last adventure to date was to become a commissionaire (on a temporary basis) at Harrods.

He is greedy, rather a snob, is always in the right (or so he thinks!) and runs a respectable Teddy Bears' Lodging House in Chelsea. The inhabitants are treated rather menially, but Bully has a kind of endearing naiveté and naughtiness which have made him popular with readers (both young and old). He is very proud of a scarf which Rupert Bear gave him when he visited Rupert's Grotto at Selfridges one Christmas, and he sits glaring across the room at Aloysius, who has a fez and a scarf given to him by Mrs Anthony Andrews which is the height of chic.

Smokey Bear

After the appearance of the cartoon of the President refusing to shoot the bear, the US Department of Agriculture adopted this cub as the national symbol for Forest Fire Prevention and called it Smokey. Two generations later, in 1950, the bear was succeeded by another cub at the Washington Zoo. Three years later the Ideal Toy Corporation, by a special Act of Congress, obtained permission to make models of Smokey and thus the American Junior Forest Fire Ranger Service was initiated.

Although not strictly a Teddy Bear, I consider Smokey an Honorary one because of the wonderful work he has done. The second Smokey retired in 1975, and has gone to live at the Ghost Ranch on the Carson National Forest in New Mexico.

A Smokey Bear Historical State Park has been established at Capitan, near the Lincoln National Forest where Old Smokey was rescued as a badly burned orphaned cub from a forest fire in 1950. Some Rangers died in this incident and the national press gave the whole thing a wide coverage.

In Memoriam Clifford Berryman 1869–1949

Clifford Berryman, much loved cartoonist for the *Washington Star* for forty years, drew the original 'Teddy Bear' cartoon above in 1902 (see pages 4–5), which probably started off the entire Teddy Bear mystique. The bear subsequently appeared in all his cartoons of Theodore Roosevelt and became a symbol associated with Berryman's signature. The day after he died the cartoon on the right by Herblock appeared.

57

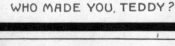

WHO MADE YOU, TEDDY?

Teddy Bear postcards

In olden days, when television, the radio and even the cinema were totally unavailable for entertainment, the showing of postcards to one another was high on the list of ploys to Keep the Guest Amused. Elaborate panoramic views in a sort of 3-D were obtained by looking through a slide viewer. It is quite easy to see how the fad grew. One-upmanship came in with a wallop, and postcards of far-off places enjoyed great popularity.

I have been collecting postcards for many years and was, I am proud to claim, instrumental in getting that fabulous comedian Ronnie Barker hooked on it. I gave him twelve postcards which, when assembled, became a picture of Napoleon. He now has thousands and thousands, and rumour has it that he moves his family from house to house to accommodate his collection, which is assembled in those marvellous old-fashioned albums. Every year he brings out a selection of his best prizes in book form, which have proved wonderful Christmas presents.

Funnily enough, neither he nor I got hold of many Teddy Bear postcards. But luckily for us Mrs Rose Wharnsby did. On pages 58-65 you will find some magnificent examples from her hoard. It has been an appalling job selecting them as she has well over thirteen hundred. Mrs W. even runs a Newsletter and a well-supported flurry of Furry Friends, called FFF, of which Aloysius, Theodore and Bully are members. She also collects Teddies themselves and if any reader wants to contact her, they can do so at 119 Linden Avenue, Ruislip, Middlesex, England.

Incidentally Theodore has asked me to point out that he was made a member of the Picture Postcard Monthly Junior Club and on his Membership card it reads 'Valid until Forever'. He's very keen on this. And rightly!

ACCIDENTS WILL HAPPEN!

HOW OFTEN · AM · I · TO · TELL · YOU · TO · PUT · YOUR · PAWS · IN · YOUR · LAP.
& NOT · GROWL · TILL · YOU'RE · GROWLED · TO ?

I WISH YOU WERE A SOLDIER, TEDDY.

WHEN FATHER TEDDY SAYS "TURN" WE ALL TURN

WAITING FOR FATHER XMAS

IF FOR A SMOKE YOU
. ARE .
INCLINED

Just Strike a Match
on the Bear behind.

RAILWAY STATION

TIME IS MONEY!

A HELPING HAND TO A STRAY

This drawing was presented by the Artist to Dr. Barnardo's Homes.

When girls go out to parties
they like a bit of fun,
Aint some Teddies awful slow,
Once they get a Bun.

HER LAST RESOURCE.

I'M LONGING FOR SOMEONE TO LOVE ME.

"I love you dear" says Teddy
"Far better than my life"
"So make me happy
sweetheart"
And say
you'll be
my wife.

A "Teddy Bear" for
the Kaiser!

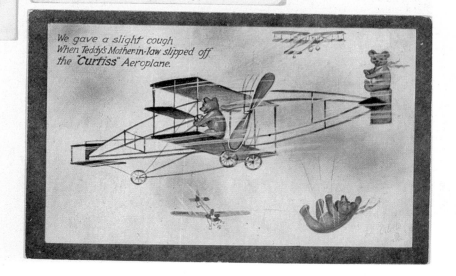

TEDDY BATHING

TEDDY-BOYS SAILING.

TEDDY AT GOLF

"THE ICE BEARS BEAUTIFULLY."

A heavy trial.

Rallies and picnics

It is only in the last fifteen years that great and small gatherings of Teddy Bear lovers have been taking place. Or perhaps I should say, attracting attention. Now not a week goes by without a celebration of some kind somewhere and I have been present and, indeed, officiated at many of them. One reason for their popularity is that it has been proved beyond doubt they are the quickest and most attractive way to raise money for charity, and their appeal to all as a Family Event is undeniable.

Possibly the first indication of all this emerged at the little village of Brundhall in Norfolk, England, in 1970 (population at that time 2,574).

(left) *Aloysius, Bully and Dolomite Daisy in a hug with friends*

TOP *The Marquess of Bath with Ian Botham's teddy (left) and Margaret Thatcher's 'Humphrey'*

BRING YOUR BEAR!

LONGLEAT
SUNDAY MAY 27th
THE GREAT TEDDY BEAR RALLY
and HONEY FAIR

LONGLEAT HONEY FAIR

TO THE GREAT LONGLEAT TEDDY BEAR RALLY

LONGLEAT — WARMINSTER — WILTSHIRE (between Bath & Salisbury on the A362) Telephone: Maiden Bradley 551

A carnival was held there to raise funds for the local Memorial Hall. Teddy Bear Competitions were one of the attractions and around fifteen hundred Teddies and the people they owned turned up.

On the opposite side of the globe, in the same year, in Auckland, New Zealand, two thousand students attended a giant lunch-time T.B. Picnic at a former Government House.

'But what do you *do* at these affairs?' I am constantly asked.

Well, to start with, there should be competitions. Every organizer has different ideas as to how these should

Bear Day at London Zoo

be divided into classes. The most popular are the Oldest, the Best-Dressed, the Largest, the Smallest, the Most Operated On, and the Teddy Looking Most Like His or Her Owner. When I went to Australia a few years ago, quite apart from the attempt by the Koalas to pretend they were Teddy Bears there was fierce competition to win the splendid prizes presented by 'Legacy', who organized the whole thing. A child whose loved friend had failed to win the Best-Dressed class disappeared behind the platform and I saw him and his

mother ripping off the lovely clothes and sticking Band-Aid plasters all over his body to qualify him for the Most Operated On Bear.

On another occasion, this time in Britain, a very bizarre-looking creature was presented for my inspection. For once I was speechless. 'He's had a transplant,' said the owner cheerfully. 'Oh,' I replied. 'Yes,' went on the lady, 'our dog bit his head off and my husband, who is a policeman, made him a new one out of some canvas and an old fur coat of mine.' So I invented a new class for the Teddy with the Best Head Transplant.

The two Rallies at Longleat set the pattern for the subsequent ones all over the world. The Stately Home, its vast grounds and the participation of the Marquess of Bath and his family made it a perfect venue. Zoos have been another popular choice and Philadelphia and London Zoos have held Teddy Happenings. Among my favourites (I must tread delicately here) was the first Longleat Rally in 1979. 'Arctophilia Runs Amok' was the headline of the full page in *Time* Magazine by its astonished reporter. Then there was the *Teddy Tribune* one at Minneapolis/St Paul (now an annual event) which brought together the most fascinating collection of arctophiles I've ever seen assembled. It was open to the public for only one day, and the crowds broke all records. At another charming, smallish affair at the London Toy and Model Museum, the highlight was an outdoor miniature railway which carried Teddy Bear passengers throughout the day.

ABOVE NSPCC *Centenary Rally, Liverpool*

OPPOSITE ABOVE *Timsbury, in aid of the National Children's Homes*

BELOW *Stratford-on-Avon*

Some of these occasions are, I fear, less well organized than others. Attendance is frequently under-estimated and children have been separated from their Teddies for too long (fatal, particularly if the latter have been heaped in an untidy muddle according to their class), and these Rallies are usually run by people who don't understand the whole mystique of Teddy Bear lovers. What they must take for granted at the outset is that the owners want more than anything to show their friends off to everyone, convinced that Theirs is the Best of All, however battered, wounded, home-made or even dirty he may be.

Good Bears of the World

I am indebted to that doyen of arctophiles, Colonel Henderson, for his concise history of this organization: its aims, its achievements, and its ideals. The British and American branches differ substantially in their format, but both have contributed hugely to the understanding and goodwill which has enriched and permeated the Teddy Bear World in the last two decades.

As Bob Henderson sees it, G.B.W. (as I shall refer to the Good Bears of the World from now on) has the prime purpose of investigating fully the phenomenon of Teddy Bear awareness, so as to liberate all people who experience it from fear of derision, and to harness their activities into a co-ordinated network of benevolent activity.

This admirable movement evolved out of the intuitive impulses of six people, all of Scottish descent, half of whom were called Henderson! Yet all six were totally unrelated, and widely separated geographically. The chronological diary of development was as follows.

1951. Russell McLean of Lima, Ohio, who had spent a great deal of his life in hospitals, started a scheme, in conjunction with a local radio station, by which Teddy Bears were given to children on their first night in hospital. He died in 1969 after presenting to children a total of 60,000 bears.

1953. Betty McDermid of New York and her bear 'Shad' (short for

Colonel Robert Henderson

Shadrack) started a voluminous and far-reaching correspondence with innumerable Teddy people, cheering and making life more fun for them.

1955. Colonel Henderson, on retiring from the Army to Edinburgh, started to research the influence of the Teddy bear in Western Society.

1962. Colonel Henderson was nominated 'President of the Teddy Bear Club' by Mrs Mimi Wands of Edinburgh, who had a large Teddy Bear as a mascot in an old peoples' home.

1964. Mrs Helen Henderson of Montreal, Canada, started to make Teddy Bears in aid of Childrens' Hospitals and other organizations in Canada. At the last count she had made 2,694. She says she loves every one of her creations equally. She is now 82.

1966. Sheena Henderson, an officer in the Salvation Army at Annan, Dumfriesshire, in Scotland,

Mrs Helen Henderson

formed a local Teddy Bear Club for children under school age.

1968. *Bear With Me* by Peter Bull was first published in Britain.

1970. The same book, under the title *The Teddy Bear Book*, was brought out in the States. General interest in the subject was aroused by these volumes in both countries, and the phenomenon of Teddy Bears settled more firmly in the awareness of the general public. Adult arctophiles came out of their closets, and in 1973 'The Teddy Bear Club' suddenly assumed a formal status. This was largely due to the efforts of an enterprising and successful broadcaster and roving reporter called Jim Ownby, based in Hawaii. He got together with Colonel Henderson and founded G.B.W. in Berne, Switzerland – an appropriate location, as the symbol for the city is a bear, and the very sound of the two words suggests a connection.

G.B.W. was established as an international humanitarian association, pledged to buy Teddies for sick children in hospitals and/or those of any age in need of psychotherapy. In the last ten years research has proved that, by reason of his increasing popularity and universal appeal, 'Teddy is a traditional object that functions as a representative of an archetypal symbol in the form of a bear'. It can be said that the G.B.W. movement exercises a new and enlightening influence amid the trials and tribulations of modern life.

Mrs Wrist, who is known as the Teddy Lady of Kingston-on-Thames, never stops making bears for charity and is a prominent member of G.B.W. A victim of Nazi oppression, she managed to escape with her sewing machine and a white Teddy called Maxie. The latter served with Mrs Wrist in the British ATS during the war. A familiar figure through frequent talks about Teddies at Womens' Clubs and on television, Mrs Wrist is pictured here with some of her handiwork.

There are now G.B.W. dens all over Britain and America, and it is up to arctophiles all over the world

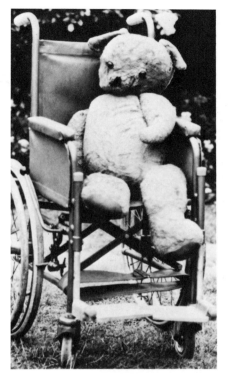

to carry on the wonderful work started by Russell McLean and others. A fascinating publication, *Bear Tracks*, the official organ of the G.B.W., is published on both sides of the Atlantic. The addresses of the Headquarters if you (or your Teddy) feel like becoming a Good Bear of the World are listed at the end of this book.

LEFT *This bear is waiting to comfort the owner of the wheelchair. The photograph was used as a fund-raising advertisement for Action Research for the Crippled Child*

BELOW *Annette Meldrum with Mrs Wrist and friends*

Teddy Tribune

News and Views of the Bear World   January 1983 Vol. IV No.

2,838 Teddies Attend Minnesota Zoo Picnic

When the picnic guests arrived at the Minnesota Zoo they were asked, "How many adults? How many children? How many teddy bears?" When the numbers were added up at the end of the day, 7008 humans had passed through the zoo gates and 2,838

bears were at the giving was to ear Picnic at the

ed by Cub Foods each person who a teddy bear. All e admitted free of ys admitted free nt, each bear f attendance and veral contests. judging in the ggest Bear, sed Bear, Best Bear Feet, Human/Bear Look-

ok-a-Like contest Some children came to look like some bears came e human. The who wore a dark s face painted carried. ntered the Teddy Bear Talent Contest. These bears brought along human assistants for their acts. Some entries were a bear who played the piano using the stage name Ludwig Van

Dorothy Molstad, zoo promotions manager, presiding over the bear contests.

Crowds of teddies and humans awaiting a decision in the bear contest.

The editorial staff (including Mrs Wolters) are under so much pressure from Dumper that they are considering joining a union (not closed shop, of course)

(continued on next page)

The Teddy Tribune

One of the most remarkable and worthwhile achievements in the Teddy Bear World is the work of Barbara Wolters, a young lady of diminutive stature but enormous energy. She started up a magazine called *The Teddy Tribune* about four years ago, which went straight to the hearts and indeed homes of every arctophile.

Not only was it crammed with news of Rallies, Conventions and Teddy Bear lovers all over the world, but it was written with such wit and heart that it appealed to every age group and avoided the sentimentality and whimsy sometimes attendant on such enterprises. It even had an agony column for Bear Pen Pals.

The Editor is a formidable Teddy called Dumper. He, Barbara and Barbara's mother run the whole thing in, luckily, a large house, situated in St Paul, Minnesota. I say luckily, because I have never seen so many bears massed in one private building. For the last three years *The Teddy Tribune* has organized a Convention, a model for such occasions, quite apart from the feeling and warmth that permeated the whole affair. The magazine started with about four pages and now has fifty-two at least.

Please pass the salt

The three solid silver cruet containers (top) were given me by my friend Robert Morley and his wife Joan on my sixtieth birthday. We have known each other for about fifty years and for me it has been a most delightful and deeply rewarding relationship. Last summer we were standing by his swimming pool in the little changing hut without a stitch on. Robert looked at his fine frame and then at mine: 'Oh Bully dear', he murmured, 'if only Rubens was still alive!'

The two lower numbers were given me by Jean Hardwicke who loves people and cats.

On the opposite page is an assortment of Beariana. There is a plate, a teapot, a bell, a glass pestle and mortar, and a receptacle for honey. The teapot was given me by James Wellman and David Swift who run a remarkable 'Theatre Room' in an old monastery near Evesham in Worcestershire, England. It provides superb food, everyone dresses to the nines and I was allowed to do my 'Evening of Bull' there.

On page 76 you will see some sporting Teddies. The adventurous balloonist was sent me by Jeannie Miller of 'Care of Your Teddy' fame, who seems to have lost her head this time. The two plates were given me by the actress Polly James, who rather surprisingly found them in New Zealand. I gave her my largest bear 'Terry' when she married the actor, Clive Francis. The badges (page 77) are, I hope, self-explanatory. If anyone disagrees with this statement they had better write to me c/o my publishers enclosing a stamped addressed envelope. This might bring elucidation though I doubt it. The bear at the bottom left on page 78 is 'preserved in ice'.

Ladies with their bears

Peggy Young (right) with just some of her hug, who live in Ardmore, Oklahoma. In 1983 she organized a rally for the B.I.M.A. (the Bears in Miniature Association), an offshoot branch of an idea of Mark Steele, who has the New Zealand Teddy Bear situation under his paw. B.I.M.A. is open to representatives who are nine inches high or less. I was invited to send one and so Terra was dispatched in cotton wool. He is made of terra cotta by Margaret Ballard and sits in an armchair very cosily, which makes travel comparatively easy.

Jean Wright (above), for many years in charge of the Children's Library at Ashford in Kent. In 1972 she ran an exhibition there called 'A Hug of Bears' (she kindly let me pinch the name for this book). An incredible number of bears attended, and the occasion was celebrated by the publication of a booklet by Miss Wright with the same title, which listed every bear book in print. The exhibition set off a whole spate of similar functions in libraries and elsewhere. 'A Hug of Bears' was reprinted in 1976.

Mrs Howard Hamilton (below) with her two daughters, Catherine and Bessie, and a few of her vast collection of Teddies. It may be recalled by ardent arctophiles that Mrs H.H., after her wedding, had a sensational going-away hat, which had two small bears perched happily on the brim. Several others were among her bridal attendants. Mrs Howard Hamilton is very prominent in the social life of Virginia and her hug participate. They all live in a house called 'Jumping Branch'.

Loved bears

As ALL BEARS are loved, or certainly deserve to be, here are just a few which we shall not name because all the *other* Loved Bears will have their snouts put out of joint – and that would be unforgivable.

Miss Fenton

In order to avoid being attacked by the Bearesses' Liberation lot, we thought it prudent to include at least one big picture of a lady bear, Miss Fenton.

There are in fact a great many dotted around the world. Colonel Henderson's 'Teddy Girl' has achieved wide fame. The Colonel is very proud of his 1903 Teddy whom he calls his Mark One Model. The bear, who is two years older than his owner, started life as the property of his elder brother, and then was shared by the two boys. Later he was inherited by the Colonel's daughter, Cynthia, and changed his sex because the girl insisted on dressing him in a frilly skirt.

Most lady Teddies are called Theodora or Tedwina. But now we have a lot of them called after famous people. Anyone from Amelia Ehrhart to Sarah Bernhardt.

But for me Teddies are curiously sexless and I would rather they remained so. However, Miss Fenton is so pretty and disarming that I thought she looked as if she were waiting for Teddy Right to come along.

Perhaps Miss Fenton will be lucky enough to catch the bouquet of the bride opposite

Small but distinguished

A few of my seemingly younger friends. On the sofa (left) is H.H. who arrived in an aluminium soap-box from a lady who simply put her initials at the bottom of a note sent with him. He had been in a sewing-basket for fifty years and needed a change. The two jointed and clothed Teddies in costume were given me by Joan Greenwood, the actress. Sitting against the sofa is Crotchety, so called because he was crotcheted (if that's the word) by the writer Cynthia Lindsay's grandmother. He is in his early seventies. Two of the littlest ones were hand-made by Elisabeth Edes, one of the best-known miniature bear makers in America. Sitting proudly on the right is a small replica of Bully Bear, given me by April Whitcomb at the New York Toy Fair of 1983. An exquisite example of the kind of work in which she specializes.

Fairly senior citizens

A little group of Teddies who, though parted from their previous owners by death or other circumstances, have managed to settle down with us.

Reading roughly from left to right: Dolomite Daisy, obtained in the Austrian Tyrol many years ago by the late Suriya Misso; Teddy, who was nearly drowned in a flood in Washington State, and who belongs to one of my partners, Don Busby; and a bear who belonged first to Pamela Brown, a superb actress and wonderful friend, then to her sister Nancy Home, and was finally passed on to me. The one with the ribbon across his chest is Grunter, to whom I referred in the introduction and about whose future his owner, aged eighty, was worried; and back row, extreme right, is an incredibly cheerful semi-invalid, brought to me by a lady from Southampton.

YOU'LL SOON BE WELL AGAIN."

Care of your Teddy

This page is really more for adults than children because, although the latter may and do care tremendously for their Teddies, they don't often give them the attention and maintenance they need. In fact, quite the reverse, and in their opinion a bear should show signs of wear and tear and being excessively loved. But it's essential that the Teddy doesn't fall apart and Jeannie Miller, who really knows what she is talking about, has sent me the following tips:

'I have found that a really top upholstery fabric cleaner is the best way to restore your Teddy to his or her pristine beauty. Just follow the instructions on the label and don't leave it on too long. When you fuss the foam into the fabric itself, then buff it off dry with a nice, heavy soft clean towel. Then he should have a warm place to dry, a sunny window or a pre-warmed oven (with the heat turned off).

'They all need a brisk brushing but with a soft-bristled brush. The bears tell me they feel much better for this invigorating experience. Be sure to get those yarn noses clean with a toothbrush and brighten those eyes with a tiny damp cloth so their visions will remain clear.

'Peter, whenever a new bear comes into our house he goes with me to the sewing chair. I carefully put a very slim crochet hook on the end, beside every seam, and pull out tucked-in fur that careless sewers miss. I usually clip the fur even

throughout, especially on the nose area. It's amazing how many bears can't see too well through somebody's inefficiency and many a lovely smile mouth remains hidden until nipped and trimmed.'

Got the message? Mrs Miller, whose address is listed at the end of the book, is a Licensed Appraiser of Antiques and Fine Arts and specializes in old Teddies. She is also a Collector and Lecturer.

A mixed bag of useful information

SURGERIES FOR TEDDIES IN NEED OF ATTENTION

Great Britain

Bristol Dolls' Hospital (Stanley Brown and Ruby Hudd), Alpha Road, Southville, Bristol

Mrs Claire Dodds, 8 Dairy Court, Birch Lane, Oldbury/Warley, West Midlands B68 ONZ

Minutiques (J. and C. Jackman), 82b Trafalgar Street, Brighton BN1 4EB

Mrs Denton-Rich, Little Shambles, Church End, Gamlingay, Cambridgeshire

The Dolls' Hospital, 16 Dawes Road, London SW6 (joints and glass eyes only)

USA

The Dolls' Hospital, 787 Lexington Avenue, New York, NY 10021

Enchanted Valley Dolls' Hospital and Bear Refuge, 1700 McHenry Village Way, Apt 5, Modesto, California 95350

The Grizzlies (Mesdames Lowery and Hixon), 223 W. Lloyd St, Pensacola, Florida 32501

Anne Rees, 161 Primrose Way, Palo Alto, California 94303

Elisabeth Edes, 8 Ridgeway East, Scarsdale, N.Y. 10583

Dr S. Stern BD, Box 258-3, Sherwood, Oregon 97140

Dr Lois Beck BD, 103000 Champaigne Lane, S.E. Portland, Oregon 97266

Margaret Mett, 601 Taneytown Road, Gettysburg, Pennsylvania 17325

Dr Dorothy Bordeaux, Rt 2, Box 760, Silver Springs, Florida 32688

GOOD BEARS OF THE WORLD HEADQUARTERS

For information about subscriptions and local den addresses in Great Britain write, enclosing a stamped addressed envelope, to G.B.W. (U.K.), 17 Barnton Gardens, Edinburgh EH4 6AF

For the United States G.B.W. write, enclosing an International Stamp Money Order, to P.O. Box 8236, Honolulu, Hawaii 96815

The G.B.W. Magazine _Bear Tracks_ can be obtained from the two addresses above.

MAGAZINES DEALING EXCLUSIVELY WITH THE TEDDY BEAR WORLD

The Teddy Bear and Friends, Hobby House Press, 900 Frederick Street, Cumberland, Maryland 21502

The Arctophile, c/o Bear In Mind, 73 Indian Pipe Lane, Concord, Massachusetts 01742

The Teddy Tribune, 254 W. Sidney Street, St Paul, Minnesota 55107

The Grizzly Gazette, 8622 East Oak Street, Scottsdale, Arizona 85257

Bear Hugs, The Hug Corporation, 300 East 40th St, NY 10016

MUSEUMS WHERE TEDDIES MAY BE VIEWED

Great Britain

LONDON

The London Toy and Model Museum, 23 Craven Hill, London W2

Pollocks Toy Museum, 1 Scala Street, London W1

The Bethnal Green Museum, Cambridge Heath Road, London E2

BRIGHTON

The National Toy Museum, The Royal Pavilion, Art Gallery and Museums (part of the collection is housed at The Grange, Rottingdean, a few miles away)

WAREHAM

The Wareham Bears, 18 Church Street, Wareham, Dorset

WORTHING

The Worthing Museum

EDINBURGH

The Museum of Childhood, 38 High Street, Edinburgh, Scotland

A private collection of great interest can be viewed by writing to *Mrs Helen MacKinnon* or her daughter, Deirdre, at Silver Trees, Scamill, West Kilbride, Ayrshire, Scotland

USA

The only collections I know of are private ones:
Mrs Iris Carter, West Locust Hill, Ivy, Virginia 22945

Mrs Jeanne Miller, Rocking Horse Ranch, Peavinnette Road, Route 3, Box 323 McMinnville, Oregon 97128

The Carrousel Museum collection, Midland, Michigan

The Roosevelt Bears may be seen at Woodford Landing Antiques, Midway, Kentucky

But I believe there are some Teddies at the *Children's Museum* in Indianapolis, P.O. Box 3000, Indianapolis, Indiana 46206, at the *Margaret Strong Collection*, Manhattan Square, Rochester, NY 14607, and at *The Atlantic Toy Museum*, 1 Peachtree Street, Atlanta, Georgia

Australia

There is a *Teddy Museum* at 118 Edward Street, Brisbane, Queensland 40000

Keeping fit – but the fur begins to fly at four-all in the final set

Acknowledgements

Appreciation and thanks are due to the following owners and photographers for the use of illustrations:

page
4 Photo: Derrick Witty
6 (*above*) Vera London
7 (*above*) John Pitt DSC
9 Pauline McMillan. Photo: Derrick Witty
10–11 St Paul's Junior School, Rusthall, Tunbridge Wells. Photos: Derrick Witty
12 Adalin Wichman
13 Mrs Howard Fenton
14 From *Summoned by Bells* by kind permission of Sir John Betjeman and John Murray (Publishers) Ltd
15 (*above*) Clarissa and James Mason (*below*) Barbara Cartland
16 (*above*) *Sesame* Magazine and Mizue Hotta
17 (*above*) Heather Chasen and Amanda Barrie (*below*) Tina Slater
18 Matt Murphy
19 Sybil Sanderson
20 Mark Steele. Photo: Tim Steele
21 The MacKinnon Collection
22–3 The Wareham Bears (Mr and Mrs Hildesley)
24 Evelyn Lovell Collection, Versailles, Kentucky. Photos: Bill Rodgers Jr
25 Virginia Walker
26 (*above, below left*) Gerald Durrell OBE (*below right*) Alan Thomas
27 Ann Cameron Seigal
28–9 Carrousel Museum Collection, Michigan
30 Martin Hayward
31 Markéta Luskačová
32 *Sesame* Magazine and Mizue Hotta
33–5 Photos: Derrick Witty
36 *The Mail on Sunday*, YOU Magazine
37 The Marquess of Bath. Photo: Lord Christopher Thynne
38–9 © Express Newspapers PLC
40, 43 (*right*) Illustrations from *The House*

page
at *Pooh Corner* Copyright E.H. Shepard under the Berne Convention. In the USA Copyright 1928 by E.P. Dutton & Co. Inc. Copyright renewal © 1956 by A.A. Milne. Reproduced by permission of Curtis Brown Ltd, London, and E.P. Dutton Inc., New York
42 Illustration from *Winnie The Pooh* Copyright E.H. Shepard under the Berne Convention. In the USA Copyright 1926 by E.P. Dutton & Co. Inc. Copyright renewal 1954 by A.A. Milne. Reproduced by permission of Curtis Brown Ltd, London, and E.P. Dutton Inc., New York
41 (*left*), 43 (*left*) Sketches from *The Pooh Sketchbook* copyright © 1979 by Lloyds Bank Ltd and Colin Anthony Richards, Executors of the Estate of E.H. Shepard and copyright © 1982 Lloyds Bank Ltd and Colin Anthony Richards, Executors of the Estate of E.H. Shepard, and the E.H. Shepard Trust. Reproduced by permission of Curtis Brown Ltd, London, and E.P. Dutton Inc., New York
41 (*right*) Brian Sibley
44 (*left, above right, below right*) © William Collins/Peggy Fortnum 1961, 1970, 1960. Thanks also to Michael Bond and his daughter, Karen Jankel
(*centre*) Central Photographic Unit, British Railways Board
45 Mary Batchelor
46–7 Teddy Edward Enterprises (Patrick and Mollie Matthews)
48–9 R.W. Weekes Ltd, Tunbridge Wells
50 Reproduced from VOGUE © Condé Nast Publications. Photo: Christopher Sykes
51 Granada Television Ltd
52 (*above right*) Granada Television Ltd (*below*) *TV Times*
53 (*above*) Granada Television Ltd

page
53 (*right and below left*) Keith McMillan
54 Enid Irving
55 *Sesame* Magazine and Mizue Hotta
56 US Department of Agriculture, Forest Service
57 (*left*) The *Washington Star* (*right*) © 1949 by Herblock in *The Washington Post*. Thanks also to the Evelyn Lovell Collection and Florence Berryman
58–65 Rose Wharnsby Collection. Photos: Derrick Witty
66 Photo: Derrick Witty
67 (*above right*) Times Newspapers Ltd (*below*) Pauline McMillan
68 (*above*) National Children's Homes (*left*) The London Zoo (Joan Crammond)
69 (*above*) NSPCC, Liverpool (Joan Gregory)
70 (*above*) Colonel Robert Henderson (*below*) Mrs Helen Henderson
71 (*above*) Action Research for the Crippled Child (*below*) © *Surrey Comet*. Photo: John Goodman
72–3 Mrs Wolters and Barbara Wolters
74–8 Photos: Derrick Witty
79 (*above*) Peggy Young (*left*) Jean Wright (*below*) Mrs Howard Hamilton
84 Mrs Howard Fenton
85–8 Photos: Derrick Witty
89 Photo: Jane Bown
90 Rose Wharnsby Collection
91 (*above right*) Mrs Jeanne Miller (*below right*) Rose Wharnsby Collection
94 America Hurrah Antiques, New York City
96 (*left*) Photo: Derrick Witty (*right*) Rose Wharnsby Collection

The Lines from 'Archibald' on page 11 are reproduced from *Uncollected Poems* by kind permission of Sir John Betjeman and John Murray (Publishers) Ltd

Good Night